Midnight River

Midnight River

~

Laura L. Hansen

Selected as winner of the National Federation of State Poetry Societies
2015 Stevens Manuscript Competition
by Bruce Dethlefsen

NFSPS Press

This publication is the 2015 winner of the National Federation of State Poetry Societies Stevens Poetry Manuscript Competition, an annual competition with a deadline of October 15th. Complete rules and information on the purchase of past publications may be obtained by visiting NFSPS at www.nfsps.com.

NFSPS Press

Cover photograph, "Ripples on My Pond at Night," by Russell Sharon
Author photo by Joey Halvorson
Cover and interior book design by Diane Kistner
Book set in Adobe Garamond Pro

ISBN 978-0-990908-22-7

Copyright © 2016 Laura L. Hansen
All rights reserved

No part of this work may be reproduced or transmitted in any form or by any means, electronic or mechanical, including photocopying or recording, or by any information storage or retrieval system except as may be expressly permitted by the publisher, *the National Federation of State Poetry Societies.*

On *Midnight River* by Laura L. Hansen:

These poems by Laura Hansen in *Midnight River* are what great poetry is and what great poetry does right. Here are word pictures painted perfectly with the most careful attention to image and sound.

Hansen's art lies in the personal and universal details: a screen door incessantly banging when no one is home ("The Plot of Land"), a "wildflower dazzling in the shorn grass like a bit of spilled wine, a drop of claret" ("A Week on Madeline Island"), fireflies in a mason jar ("See the Child") and the steel wool water ("Midnight River").

I would read these poems to someone I love, slowly, by the fire, on an endless November Sunday afternoon.

—Bruce Dethlefsen, Wisconsin Poet Laureate (2011-2012)

Judge's notes on the 2015 winning manuscript of the National Federation of State Poetry Societies Stevens Manuscript Competition

*Dedicated to my father
who stands watching at the shore.*

Contents

Chapter One | Beauty, solemn

Renewal... 13
Cedar Waxwings.. 14
aftermath.. 15
The Message.. 16
Beauty, solemn.. 17
A Tree Snaps... 18
The Leaf.. 19
Aspiration... 20
If I Named You... 21
The Generous Ones.. 22
See the Child... 23
Blue Rain, Yellow Day.. 24
Down There.. 25
Trincomalee.. 26
The Pleasure of Rain... 28
Passing Thoughts.. 29

Chapter Two | Other Rooms

Be Happy... 33
Infield Afternoon.. 34
Scribbage... 35
Picture from a Trip... 36
Perfect Is As.. 37
Mother's Day at the Nursing Home............................. 38
Mother's Feet.. 40
The Wheelchairs... 41
Other Rooms.. 42
The Plot of Land... 43
Rough Cut.. 44
At the Museum... 45
Opening Up.. 46
What Holds Me.. 47

Last Pocket 48
Benediction 49

Chapter Three | Wind /shadow

Destroying Angel 53
Wind /shadow 54
Off the Map 55
A Week on Madeline Island 56
Poem in Which No Bird Appears 57
At Noma Lake 58
Glove Lake Morning II 59
Just Now a Fish 60
Reunion Moon 62
Night Burning 63
Wolves in the Night 64
Why I Keep Rabbits 65
Spitting on Stones 66
No Regrets 67

Chapter Four | Renewal

Putting By 71
Last Train Song 72
Migraine 73
Larger Than Life 74
At the Exhibit 75
Bakery Fresh 76
Poem for Pablo 77
The Poem as Trickster 78
This Is the Poem 79
Digging for Truth 80
Munitions 81
A Good Night 82
Midnight River 83
Tomorrow the Real Work Begins 84

Chapter One | *Beauty, solemn*

Renewal

I watch the terns' slow dance,
how they move on the breath
of the wind, and know

where tenderness begins.

Cedar Waxwings

They come only once or twice a year,
swarming like bees, one always

in the air while another feeds,
so many of them that

the air shivers. We feel the pulse
of their wings from ten feet away,

feel it just inside the door
where we have suspended

our sawing, our typing, our reading,
suspended all but the gift of belief.

They swarm the smallish tree, greedy
in the cold spring air, for the bruised

berries that have gone unnoticed
all winter, gobbling them as if

a little drunk, a little giddy
with pleasure, nonetheless

moving in and out and around
with absolute precision, the little

leafless tree grown huge
with their whirring and darting

and hovering presence, and us grown small
in the face of their insatiable appetite.

aftermath

crush a wild raspberry
    between your fingertips
        you are bleeding

red juice sluices
    as from
        an unrepentant wound

drips off your finger
    and splashes
        suddenly thin

onto a wild ginger leaf

crush a wild raspberry
    between your fingertips
        raise it to your lips

red juice stains
    the toe of your boots,
        the laces, your chin

later you will remember
    the red sting of sweetness
        the puckering green of shame

The Message

Drop a leaf
in the current

and it will
surely pass my way.

You and I live
in the same place,

in the shallows
and sandbars,

in the sweeping arc
of the river's bend,

in those reeds
on the opposite shore

where pelicans
patiently circle,

hoeing their long chins
through the waves

sifting the sediment
for news.

Beauty, solemn

and black as a rifle's barrel,
the river's steely surface sheared open

a gash, stark and glinting, stretches out
along the jagged-edged ice

a pair of ducks, crisp in black and white,
settle on the warm day's opening

heads tipped back, they catch the sun
in amber beaded eyes

a sharp caw, a frantic warning, cuts the silent day
like the crack of breaking ice

outside the window, a white tail passes, and talons follow,
the eagle flees the angry crow

sun breaks over the trees and a thumbprint of white
flares on the cheeks of the goldeneyes

as they rise on whistling wings, turning south,
away from the eagle and the sharp-tongued crow.

A Tree Snaps

In memory of Wayne Sauey

A barred owl moves through the forest
winging low past the transparent windows
of the yellow brick house,

called perhaps by the smell of wood smoke,
or by the corn shucked this afternoon on the porch,
corn culled from what little the deer left untouched.

A tree snaps in the night, constricted by cold
and a new wound opens, ragged and ready
to run with spring sap, sap that has been given

many times before to the man and the woman
who comb these woods for morels and owls
and small frozen moles and mice and ferns,

for splendid mushrooms that stretch
horizontally like shelves from the altar
of the oaks. Here she lays a stone, there

she places a bi-colored leaf,
at another she stops and places
the remains of her heart.

A tree snaps, the owl flies,
a stone lies silent beneath the trees.

The Leaf

This fragile reddish stem
connects us, this leaf
sprinkled with cayenne red,
the edges aged and yellowing.

This act of stooping down
and picking up and clutching
beauty to our chest
connects us, this need

to clutch and carry, hold
and save, a single maple leaf
connects us, you lifting hope
from the grass,

and returning secretively
to your nursing home bed,
me, stopped on the sidewalk,
leaf in hand, remembering you.

Aspiration

The raindrop travels
the length of the tree
like a lover slipping
a moist tongue along arms,
over leaves, past bud
and seed, licking slowly
around a slender trunk,
sliding past limbs, past knees
right down to the grateful
green grass
where it catches
the emerging sunlight
in its liquid eye.

If I Named You

I saw an eagle in the sky yesterday, black wings
stretched across the blue like compass needles
pointing east and west. I saw an eagle
yesterday, but I didn't know his name.

I heard a loon cry late last night,
a hollow reed of a voice wavering
across the water. I heard the loon
twice, but I still don't know its name.

I watched a flock of waxwings swarm
the bushes outside this week, dozens
and dozens of them in their smooth
buff coats and yellow painted tails,

and I didn't know the name of a single
one. I live among people I know. I call
my dogs by name, but the wild things
are known only to their own,

their names are calls, and songs, a hoot,
a warble, a wail. They are known to
each other by scent and sound, by the lift
of a tail, a head-dipping dance.

The Generous Ones

I bundle them together, each leaf
a riot of paprika, saffron, cinnamon.

With each step down the sloping lawn,
I gather the freshest, most recently downed.

The maples give them up freely, willingly,
with quiet glee.

They are generous, these trees, unlike some
who hold on until spring, sorry brown oaks

leaves clinging, heads hung low,
through February's ice and damp heavy snow.

I bring you only the generous ones, leaves
spilled from open (uplifted) prayerful arms.

I bring them bundled and tied in thin bright ribbon,
a gift for you, a gift of the season.

See the Child

for Aunt Bernice

See her, the child, with hands cupped, chasing through the yard at dusk.
See the mason jar on the back steps, flickering against the hard red brick.
See the fireflies, signaling to their mates, scribing their love
      across the summer sky, dipping their tails into the grass like ink.

Watch the image silently play out like an old film,
jumping and flickering. The film is ratcheting through, a bit torn,
but there, there she is,
      an old mason jar put to new use.

See, see there, some child has taken the jar outside at dusk and filled it
with lightening bugs, males and females both, and now inside ideas
are blinking and sparking and the frantic flies (can you see them?)
      are bouncing off the glass trying to get out.

Blue Rain, Yellow Day

The blue bucket has been collecting rain
all week, it trembles in the sun.

I ask you to bring the blue bucket
filled to the brim

with sun and rain and pollen and
pollywogs

into the shade, to dip it slowly
over my head.

In the shade the bucket looks
almost transparent.

In the sun I look almost
happy.

You tip the rain-filled pail
until the contents

spill out in a smooth stream
and I am drenched

and laughing, shaking away
the stars from my hair,

tossing pollen across the yard,
pollywogs morphing

into frogs, frogs croaking out
the sound of joy,

a blue-bucket-filled-to-the-brim
kind of joy.

Down There

Down there I can hear said the deaf boy, the little cousin
we lost in the 30's.

He had gone swimming with us in the granite quarries
and heard a buzzing.

If I go down deeper he said in his deaf child's
underwater voice

I'll be able to hear, really hear, he said as he ran back
and dove in again.

The quarry was a deep-water place, all hard angles
and cold, so very cold,

but kids came and swam almost every
summer day.

Most came out, but Ben heard a siren's song
and stayed.

He would have stayed for most any little bit
of sound,

but he was sure if he dove deeper there
would be more,

a hearing world, a host of voices, of frogs
nattering,

birds with their marvelous songs, his mother's
voice.

Down there, in the inky cold waters of the quarry
was a voice,

her voice. The one he lost the day he
was born.

Trincomalee

for Athistarani

Dear sister, you are talking
while the television
is muted.

I hear
your soft accent
as if from another room,

roo roo roo,
round vowels
curl off your lips,

pour down
to the floor, but
never quite reach me.

I am tired
and I want to ask you
to speak to me in Tamil,

but what I think is
Sing to me.
Sing me a song.

You sit across the room
relating the details
of your day here

in Minnesota,
but what I want
is for you to tell me

about a day
in Sri Lanka
when you were a girl

like all the other girls
with your wild dark
swirls of hair

and skin soft
as ripe mango,
your voice

trickling like a
long lost melody,
a song of Trincomalee.

The Pleasure of Rain

There was a boy who noticed
the raindrops, not
the rain.
      He noticed, too,

on long grumbling days of cloud
and thunder, how all the adults
complained;
      he thought this strange.

He thought each glittering drop
that fell was beautiful.
Quietly he sat and watched
      and watched.

He tried to hold the thought of one,
one single droplet at a time,
like a painting, a picture
      in his brain,

but the droplets gathered,
shimmered, squirmed and his eyes
twitched and he was amazed,
      he shuddered,

      every time,
with the pleasure of rain.

Passing Thoughts

What I am trying not to say
passes over my face
like the smattering of shadows

that darken the sidewalk
when a flock of geese
passes overhead.

Without lifting your head
to the sky,
you understand.

Chapter Two | *Other Rooms*

Be Happy

It is in there somewhere, like that bit
of Juicy Fruit chewing gum you
accidentally swallowed back in 1984
when you tripped on the curb
you didn't notice because
you were staring up at the sky
and admiring all those geese
flying in broad bands
toward a better warmer place
and you were thinking of a trip
you might take someday
to a place where no one
would know you and you
could be anybody
somebody grand
or clever
or a woman who wears bold
colors and flimsy scarves
that catch in the wind
and holler *joie de vivre*
without you having to say a word
and you would be the one
that made people turn their heads
and lose track of where they were
and fall off curbs, swallowing
their own happiness.

Infield Afternoon

The ball moves from one to the other,
gloved hands scoop and clutch and toss,
scoop and clutch and toss, elbows bent,
knees flexed, and the stretch, quiet
reigns in the blistering afternoon sun,
the crowd mills restlessly, morose,
as the team warms up, in the stands
the pop of a can, fizz, the slap of a hand
chasing a fly, on the field, dust flares
as a ball scuds, thrown too low,
a voice from behind the dugout fence
cajoles, "keep 'em up, let's go,"
and the gloved hands toss, and scoop
and clutch, and toss and the umpire yells,
"Batter up!"

Scribbage

The dice rattle around in the cup
like a collection of missing teeth,
the black letters like deep cavities
etched into the yellowed enamel.

Inside the dice box letters tumble,
smack into each other, turn over
like wayward stars, new constellations
forming and reforming.

The dice box is tipped
and from its astonished mouth
odd bits spew out, bits of lettered
enamel, ivory, old bones and

the sudden shock of language.

Picture from a Trip

Mimi wears a floral dress in moss-soft green,
belted at the waist, somewhat baggy
as if she bought it when she weighed more
though I always remember her as being thin.

I stand beside her, my hair in a 60's pixie-cut.
I wear solid-colored shorts, a sleeveless shirt,
one my mother has held on to since the 50's,
dark anklets and white canvas tennis shoes.

We are standing in her backyard in Glendive.
My first solo trip to Montana. It is 1969 and
Mimi is in her eighties. I am not yet twelve
and yet we are like two pegs on a line.

Her hair, thin and wispy like mine, escapes
her tightly pinned bun. It swirls around
and away from her face as if seduced
by a phantom wind on a calm afternoon.

Perfect Is As

My mother and I wore
pedal pushers, crinkly seersucker pants
that stopped, abruptly, at the ankles.
We had mother-daughter dresses, too.
Pale yellow sleeveless dresses
with white piping at the waist.
Every night she would pin curl my hair,
little fingertip curls swirled
with a liberal dousing of Dippity-Doo.
And Mother tried to give me manicures,
tried to shape pretty half-moons
at the base of each of my fingernails.
She'd cut them so close they'd bleed
and then she'd say, as if it was
the most natural thing in the world,
you have to suffer to be beautiful,
you know. And now, I always
think of her that way, that
making everything painfully
perfect way.

Mother's Day at the Nursing Home

Mother yells
don't push me in the pond, don't.
I only want her to see the duck,
the lone mallard that sways slowly
around the tiny man-made pond,
the teal of his blue-green head
bluer than the water
which is thick with soft green scum
the color of peeled avocados.

I tell her she needs fresh air,
real fresh air in her lungs.
She shivers, shakes her head.
The sky is piercing blue,
but it is still cool
and we came outside without a shawl
to protect her shoulders,
no blanket to cover her aching knees
or her slipper-clad feet.

So we rattle back inside,
the wheelchair jarring
$^{ka}bump\ ^{ka}bump\ ^{ka}bump$
every three feet
where the sidewalk has heaved
like the spring roads heave
in Minnesota after a long winter.
I try to smooth her way,
to miss the biggest bumps.
Try not to look too far
down that road I am going
when my own bumpy sidewalk
will become as impassable
as the winter-rutted road
she is traveling.

Don't, she intones,
through clenched
and gritted teeth,
and again, softer,
don't.

Mother's Feet

Mother's feet
are like a planetary system
that has been knocked askew
by a passing asteroid
or comet.

The big toes, raw-meat red
from tight shoes and calluses,
wobble at the end
of their abbreviated axes.

Mother's feet
have four toes each,
the wayward little ones
surgically removed
eons ago.

The remaining toes wander
the outer reaches
of the system,
their erratic orbits crossing
at inconvenient angles.

Mother's feet
refuse to be comfortably
boxed in shoes.
They regularly riot, and yet

she loves to have them
photographed, the arcing
blues and purple bruise
of her bunions unfolding
like an aurora.

The Wheelchairs

There are too many
    They scatter

        Haphazardly
Around the room   up and down
    THE HALLS

They are a maze
    I cannot find my way
    T
     H
    R
     O
      U
     G
    H

I step carefully around one
    Bumpintoanother

I apologize, but
    The chairs
    Do not answer

Once in awhile one tells me a story
Or asks about the weather

That one holds a doll
    And this one
Is missing a leg

Sometimes I come when they are on parade

They used to frighten me, but now
I maneuver out of their way

As if I've been doing it
All my life

Other Rooms

When Thomas doubted the life he saw before him
he asked to touch Christ's wounds.

He touched his palms to Christ's pierced hands,
to his punctured side, and knew.

Standing here, looking at the place
where the chemo port enters your chest,

following the red burn of the line
as it passes into your skin,

I feel like Thomas, needing to touch
these sacred places to truly know you.

If I could, I would place a palm
to your chest, slip my finger

into your palm, aim my doubting eyes
straight into your eyes.

You've grown frailer, but more human, too
weaker and yet more god-like.

How are we to understand this transformation,
this moving so effortlessly from one room

to another?

The Plot of Land

The plot of land, exhausted.
The house, shuttered.
The cat slinks through
the ruined garden.

A screen door bangs
incessantly—
*no one's home, no one's
home, no one's
home.*

Rough Cut

Her hair, when it brushed the rough wood walls, snagged
and tensed and frizzed like a fine bit of curling ribbon.

He could see it sizzle against the walls wherever
she had bent to lift a pot or stretched to hang a scarf.

All through the fall, after she left, the cabin
continued to sprout new tendrils of her hair.

They shivered in the odd octagonal room, trembled
like his hands, pale as milk, under the October moon.

Her hair lived on through the long winter and into spring,
graying with dust and dulling as if she were growing old with him.

He carried on with the plowing, cutting, planting and hoeing.
He cut wood and built the fire and ate whatever he could muster.

But he let the windows, cracked by falling limbs and howling snow
stay cracked, the logs go un-chinked, the hand-sewn curtains tatter.

He let it all go, thinking that when it was gone to dust, he, too,
could finally go, and yet he walked the walk of the blind all night

circling the cabin and fingering each remembered place
where spun webs of her hair held firm to the wall.

He circled through the night, eyes closed, hands on the old log walls
flicking past each filament of her love, his fingers splintered and raw.

At the Museum

We circle the cabin, peer into
its broken windows and take in
the still hanging bunks, the limpid
tattered mattresses, the old wood
stove with gaping ash-filled belly
and the flannel shirt pegged
to the wall. It is all here yet—
the broken light shears through
the empty windows, spotlights
the silent artifacts, the broom,
the axe, the table, the hoe.

We like the history of abandoned
cabins, of artifacts found under grass.
We haunt un-peopled places
fraught with shattered light,
light that scatters through broken
windows like shards of glass,
places where voices of the past
whisper from the stuffing
of old mattresses, where
only trees intrude
on the growing solitude.

Opening Up

Open-palmed I lie in bed,
welcome whatever comes,
rain falls, a moth tries to smother the light
coming from the window. I breathe.
I stretch my arms wider, cup hands
as if dipping in for a drink of water
from a stream. I skim the sheets
with the toes of my restless feet.
Sleep does not come, but thoughts do,
words spoken in my father's voice.
"I worry," he says, "about all these
brothers dying." I startle awake.
Whose brothers? Mine?
Is it an oracle's pronouncement,
a premonition? How is it my yoga-
inspired meditation leads to this,
these worrisome voices,
these brief frenetic dreams?
Last night I dreamed we found
a lost dresser and an antique box.
One belonged to my father,
the other to grandpa Heddy.
We sighed with relief, pulled
open drawers, prised up the top
in search of something we were sure
we had lost, but all we found inside
were sprung suspenders, floppy and loose,
polyester ties, old underpants and socks,
inexpensive cufflinks, faux-silver flaking off.
No family jewels, no diaries.
The most significant find
was a lifetime of unopened gifts,
a bounty of unused colognes,
aftershave, soaps.

What Holds Me

What holds me together is this house
two steps up from the shore of the river;
the closets filled to overflowing

with old rubber boots and overcoats,
with knitted mittens and sleeping bags
with tents and skates and tennis rackets.

What holds me together is the weight
of the attic with its burden
of ladies' hats and boxes of too-wide ties,

with grandma's teacups and decades
of Christmas cards.
There are cards

from people I remember and names of people
I've never known.
The cards cozy up next to old photos

and report cards and family letters,
curl up on top of wedding albums
and outdated medical texts.

I recently found rolled in a corner
the posters that used to decorate my room.
I peered through the two-foot tube

as if it was a telescope to the past
and I saw Snoopy dancing and dancing
and dancing through the years

in a swirl of nostalgia and attic dust.
It is dust that holds me here, dust
that cannot be brushed away.

It adheres like a fingerprint taken
and filed, a mark that identifies me
as a prisoner of the past.

Last Pocket

In memory of my father

The green felt surface of the pool table
is pocked with tip marks, with white chalk

and some blue—we've stuffed
the torn leather pockets

with newspaper, old news
cradles every shot.

The pockets hang like oriole nests,
dried leather latticed

and flaking, beneath the banked
green lawn of the tabletop.

Red and green and yellow balls
gather in the pockets

like bright-colored birds
settling in for the evening.

You call last pocket
and the ball slams home.

The cue rattles like a fallen
branch onto the table

where only the cue ball,
near-white as snow, remains.

Benediction

To these waters, Father,
I commend your spirit,
To the river I stand before,
To all the waters that flow
Through lives and through lands.

To the dust of Montana, Father,
I commend your spirit,
To the dry hills and empty plains,
To the small towns spaced wide,
To the land of your coming,
To the land of your leaving
And the land where you are laid.

To the newborn shrieking
With the first slap of life,
I commend your spirit,
To the child with scraped knees,
To the frightened weary mother,
To those you mended, Father,
And to those you could not save.

Chapter Three | *Wind /shadow*

Destroying Angel

(Amanita virosa)

Walking into the whisky light
of dusk, our conversation
slips into neutral, then stalls.
Crickets and tree frogs
cease to *chitter*. We move
through day's last light,
breathe in the sultry smoke of dusk,
our eyes drawn down
to the ground like fingers
through the buttery light
and there, amongst the salad
of mixed leaves
between woods and road,
we see a single mushroom rise,
concave, fleshy, and pale.
In its up-stretched palm
it holds a maple leaf,
its yellow jacket sprinkled
with embers, and two pine needles,
tinder-brown. I stop and kneel
as if before a tiny altar.
I imagine a Japanese cup,
a Chinese wok, their gently
sloping forms. I see utensils,
carefully placed, and ponder
what pilgrim of the woods
has left these here: a plate of bark,
a mushroom cup, a scoop
of hollowed log.

Wind /shadow

Buffeted by an autumn wind
        as crisp
as a recently cellared apple
we crest the hill   and find ourselves
in   wind/   shadow

the gentle slope of the hill is a shoulder
we hide behind   sheltering
resting   remembering

moments ago the chill wind
and the warm sun
    played off our faces
        like sweet against sour

here in the hill's shadow
we crave   again   the sun
we lift feet
    step back   up   out of wind/

shadow
    to the pinnacle of the hill
the height   of our
    senses

Off the Map

I am a hollowed tree, a splitting oak,
feet dug in to a bit of scrubby land.

I am a shedding cattail, white-haired
and bent, on the shore of a county lake.

I am a seldom-used forestry road, all weed
and dust, an abandoned logging trail.

I am a track in the woods, stained with oil
where the 4-wheeler stopped a day or an hour ago.

I am a used-up gravel pit where teens partied
and petted last fall, leaving their mark in paint

and cans and one lost tennis shoe, the tilted
dead-end sign all pocked with gunshot wounds.

I am old and used and off the map, but
I am the place that everyone wants to go.

A Week on Madeline Island

A wildflower in the shorn grass
dazzles like a bit of spilled wine,
a drop of claret.

Another tiny flower along the path,
three oval petals no bigger
than three grains of saffron rice.

Roadsides here are lined with
Queen Anne's lace, enough to veil
the brides of Madeline for years.

Evenings the deer browse,
tourists ride bides to and from
the beach, sated with sun,

with yellow rice, and berried wine,
married—for now—to this place
dressed in lace and capped by moon.

Poem in Which No Bird Appears

In the stump of the old willow, now
flush
      with shoots the color of tamarind,
a wing flutters, pale,   diaphanous.

One triangular feather-white wing
shimmers
      in the late afternoon sun,
but no bird can be seen.

On this clearest of clear days,
a day
      without a hint of breeze
something causes the leaves

to pulse with life, to breathe,
turns
      a single willow leaf
from tree-bound-green-caterpillar

to fluttering muslin moth.
I walk outside,   pause
      in the lee of the tree
and wait for that same trickster god

to lay its hand on me.

At Noma Lake

The morning fog goes green
as it drains into the pine-shaded lake.

The campgrounds behind me
recede across the road and become

part of another time, another
century.

I sit among recently butchered
stumps of trees, sit

and take in the musk
of pine needles and moss.

The quiet is dense and alive
and I feel as if eyes

gaze on me from the past,
as if

this holy place could not exist
except in some other time

when only owls see clearly.
I rise and press my feet to the path.

Glove Lake Morning II

This morning I look down
into the shallow lip of the lake, beyond
the surface reflections, and I think

how even in this cold and rain
I am drawn down into it. How I long
to stretch my legs into a firm forceful

leap and dive in just past that rock,
touching its smooth mossy curve
with a following hand as I skim by

and slice down under its lovely
sky-reflecting invitation. The water
is a trickster, playing racing games

with cloud and wind, ripples fading
and shading, marking then hiding
along its surface brief gusts, making

a stiff chop appear like a dark
scrabbled line of scree. The water
reflects first sky, then cloud,

then pine, then disappears
completely, appearing
more transparent than glass,

leaving me to believe
I can touch the very bottom
of the lake, as if the water exists only

as the rock, the weed, the minnow,
as if loons dance upon air, dipping
their long black feet into nothing more

      than clouds.

Just Now a Fish

Just now a fish jumped out of the water.
I wonder if he is jumping up to catch
a fly, or trying to get a breath of fresh air,
or is he jumping for joy

or, maybe, the joy is an after-
thought. Maybe he jumps
for food and the joy is what he feels
as the delicate winged nymph

slips down his throat and the last
light of the sun shines briefly
in his fishy eyes before he slips
back into the tea-stained water

of the Mississippi again. I wonder
if he is a young fish, confident
in his skills and well-muscled, eyeing
the ladies as he launches himself

in a sleek glistening arc
up past the surface of the river?
And do they watch back as he
disappears with a final flick

of tail and fin up above the one-
way mirror of the water's under
edge? And if he, if it is a he,
is an older fish, I wonder will

he soon weaken, become stiff
in his aching back, unable to bend
and will he then flounder quietly
in the slow-moving shadows

below the dock, all the joyous leaping
gone, hoping for nothing more

than respite from the heat
and glare of the summer sun?

It is nearly night now and in the light
of the rising moon, fish are jumping.

Reunion Moon

The moon plays pat-a-cake with the barn, places
its benevolent palm on the silo's crown
like a blessing, an elder's benediction.

Small frogs slither through the wet-mown yard
finding nowhere to hide under the moon's
bright celebratory light.

Hay bales ring the campfire, and smoke rises
from diseased pine logs, and the hand-made violin
responds to the strumming of the guitar.

Classmates gather around like colorful gourds,
heads nodding together to a gently-strummed tune.
As the hours wind down

and stars blink on, the last few party-goers
lean in to the fire, listen to the secrets
of the whispering coals.

Night Burning

Here's the fuchsia sky and the fire
that burns all night
keeping the stars awake
and us, too, our hoods pulled up
against the chill
as we bake our toes,
black rubber boot bottoms
burning on the circled stones.

Here's the fuchsia sky,
the one that made us stop
and sit still, that begged us
to circle like the Wiccans
and balladeers
in worship around
the blue, blue fire, hands
held out in penance
to the snapping flames.

Here's the fuchsia sky,
a diva demanding to be seen, tossing
her fancy scarves across
the mirror of the lake
while we wait
in rapt attention
for the final scene.

Wolves in the Night

The dog is angling away up a steep embankment
on the other side of the river.
I call and I call but he keeps
heading farther away and up the hill.
Suddenly he turns as if to run back to me
but stops, ears perked up as a pack
of wild dogs—huge as wolves—
crest the hill behind him. He halts
and waits as they stream down the hill
with frightening speed, bounding
and scrabbling onto the river's hard
packed surface, coming my way.
Jack is still at the top of the rise—
impassive, watching. Before I know it
the first two dogs—no, now I see
they are wolves—are rushing past me
and knocking me to the side. My legs
are rooted in the deep snow, still
I reach out for balance and my fingers
skim through their bristling fur.
I struggle to right myself
and come to realize one has stopped
and is half lying on my side
pinning me down. Another, this one black,
has my ankle in his mouth holding
me in an unbreakable grip.
I wake, covered in sweat,
twisted in the sheets, something still
biting down hard, weighing me down.

Why I Keep Rabbits

They settle onto their rear
haunches and lather up
their tiny wooly front paws
with spittle, licking
as delicately as if cleaning
a newborn for the very first time,
and then they begin to wash

running their moistened paws
over their cheeks, tenderly as
a lover, tamping down their hair,
pulling gently down on their ears,
grooming themselves as fussily
as a mother tends her only child,

each movement slow and measured,
each caress a lesson in how to take care
of ourselves, how to show ourselves
love like nothing else can.

Spitting on Stones

I spit on the rock you hold out and expose
a cool blue lake, rub the film of road dust away.

You spit in the same place, take your broad thumb
and swirl away the mud of our combined spittle.

A grey-blue agate emerges, one side duff and rough,
the other a reflective pool on a windless day.

The flat edge of the stone dries in the sun, dulls,
but we know what lies inside its dense cavern.

We could take out your pocket knife and slit
our wrists, press our weeping flesh together

in an oath of blood and it would not bond us
more surely than this, our wet kisses

breathing life into this
broke-open heart of stone.

No Regrets

We've just pulled the carrots up in the garden.
They have fine yellow dangling roots, roots like stray
blonde hairs, and a nice crust of black dirt,
and tops, green tops, longer by far
than the carrots themselves.

We hold them up for you to view,
hold them in clumps of threes and fours,
hold them up in the setting sun for you to see.
Come, our eyes beg, come—there are potatoes
here, too, red and gold—Yukon—and All Blue.

Our hands tangle together, crusted in good black dirt
like the carrots, slightly ridged and hard
from a day in the garden, but pure still
under the skin, and from down on the
ground—our knees touching—we smile and smile.

Come, we say, the weeding is already done,
Come. Join us for dinner in the garden.

Chapter Four | *Renewal*

Putting By

for Kathryn Kysar

You can't feed children with nothing in the larder.
You can't grow flowers without sunshine and water.

So I am filling my fridge, feeding my belly.
I am filling the rain barrel, watering my flowers.

I am gleaning enough to boil down into syrup.
Next week or next month when I am back at work,

worrying about money and the house,
talking books and business, I will have enough

to get by, to feed my writing, to water my poems.
Something is growing in my garden.

August's work will soon be cellared and waiting.
Later, I will carry it up the slant stone steps

and hold it in its mason jar before the wintry sun.
I will let its jewel-tone light caress my face.

I'll set it on the counter, crack the lid,
let a puff of summer wind gasp out.

Then I will dip my index finger in and lift it out
dripping with maple syrup, with the waxy milk of bees,

their hard-earned pollen, with raspberries as thick
and garnet red as my own blood.

Last Train Song

I'm starting to get up at night
just to listen to their songs.
I stand in the bare moonlight,

letting their long aaah-aaah-ooo
wash over me like gentle rain.

The songs come out of the south,
a soft woo-wooing wavering
in the distance, eerie as silence,

aaah-aaah-ooo, hoo-aaah-hoo ha,
growing louder, nearer, then passing on.
Already I miss their yodeling songs,

soon they will be silenced, their night
songs banned in our town,
and only a few of us will lie awake

restless and troubled,
unable to bear the long quiet.

Migraine

Blue neon strikes like lightening
in jagged downward bursts.

Eyes closed, light
sears, buzzing electric blue,
illegible letters seen
through a window,

letters blue, obscured by rain
melt down the outside
of the window, my eyes,
I cover my eyes, and curl

into a ball in the dark
of my room, kicking blankets aside
but not the pain, neon blue
stabs again and again

like a reprimand, a back-handed
slap. *Go,* it says, *go to your room
and stay there until I can stand
to look at you again.*

Larger Than Life

Late evening
and it sounds like a S.W.A.T. team
is in the crawl space above my head
dragging and scraping along
on bellies, hands, and knees,
rifles at the ready.

Nearly midnight
and it sounds like a team of huskies
is determinedly pulling a heavy sled
across the frozen tundra
of the white ceiling tiles,
crunching and scrabbling on rough ice.

Morning
and I find the body of a smallish bat
      wings tucked in
            asleep
between the heavy folds of the drapes.

What a relief, how strange,
to find these night terrors
by the light of day
can fit in the palm of my hand.

At the Exhibit

If you touch the tall blue vase,
will it be cold in your hands?
And that tawny pot with markings
that look like stitching up its side,
will it feel like softened leather
under your curious thumb?

Will the slender urn whose glaze
swirls around it like desert dust
set off a tingling in your arms
as its sun-streaked storms
race across your palms?

Can that blackened pot
remember the moment the kiln-
heat scorched its skin, the moment
when the potter pulled it out
and brushed away the ashes,
scraped off its crusted foot?

Does the big-hipped pot
resent the slenderer one
or revel in its full belly,
its deep capacity
for wheat or oats,
for well-aged wine
or just-pressed oil?

Bakery Fresh

I like my metaphors with jelly inside,
my plot twists rolled in sugar.

My characters must never
be artificially sweetened.

I like the horror of tearing away
the golden skin and finding

the glistening jam inside.
It oozes out. I lick it in.

I have whole libraries filled
with bakery goods,

with salty syntax
and multi-syllabic sprinkles.

I have books where the pages
stick, and books where the

pages are the color of
clarified butter.

I have whole shelves
of long johns stacked end to end.

I like my reading to come
straight from the oven.

Poem for Pablo

Neruda writes of life
      as if it were
the sweet tart juice of a lemon
sucked from a rind
      whose bitterness
still presses against his lips.

The Poem as Trickster

Poem, I try to dig you out
from under the snow,
but the snow keeps falling
and you are hidden again.

Poem, I try to scoop you up
but the snow is too fine
and by the time I'm done
you are blowing across the yard.
You are laughing at me.

Poem, you are scurrying
across the neighbor's drive,
swirling around the evergreens.
I cannot catch up to you.
I cannot reach you.

Poem, I want to live in you,
burrow under your spirit drifts.
I want to shuffle along in your wake,
watch you tangle around my ankles
like long flow-y skirts.

Today, I tried to scoop a poem
from the ever-falling snow
and found
the metallic bite of defeat,
the lonely bliss of letting go.

This Is the Poem

This is the poem I cannot write.
This is the thing I cannot say.
My father died three times
last night, three times I dreamt
they took his body away.
They laid him on a gurney
at night, covered from head
to heel, they laid him on a gurney
with wheels, but didn't cover his toes.
In the second dream, I saw a white dog
out in the blistering snow, the dog
came to life and shook himself off,
but my father sat still and froze.
My father died once more last night
in a hospital room I dreamed,
my father died again last night,
and I fear there are still more dreams.
I fear the stages of grief aren't complete.
I fear the nine lives of sleep.

Digging for Truth

History is hard. It doesn't jump out at you
like a polished agate on a beach of small dark stones.

It hides deep in the sand; it disguises itself
under an unattractive mottled shell.

Even if you find it and crack it open
you can only guess at how it came to be,

how many years it took to compress
the dust of time into dimpled, banded art.

We can never really know why one is banded
and another has an array of white-centered eyes,

why some have hearts of shimmery quartz
and others shy away from reds and browns,

their insides shot through instead
with swales of blue and gunmetal gray.

Munitions

In the gunmetal sky
above the National Guard training camp,
    a squadron
is preparing to land.
Canada Geese break formation,
fan out and land in a ruckus
    of squawking,
scatter themselves
across the firing range.
They scrabble about
in the practice field, scavenging.
In fall, geese feed by day
in stubble-d corn rows, returning at dusk
to the river to rest.

These spring geese have found
    instead
this crop of spent munitions,
a landscape pocked
and cratered by shelling.
Nearby, in the Veteran's Cemetery,
    lies my father
among evenly laid rows
of identical stones that fan out
in long repeating v-s,

row after row of spent
    men.
A mile down the highway
the dead fox pillows his red head
on the edge of the road.

A Good Night

It's a good night to worship the moon. Near full
and brassy, it demands attention, commands
the sleepwalker to venture outside.

The sleepless blame the moon for midnight
wanderings, following in the footsteps of those
who walk but do not wake.

At the lunar behest
I stand outside in the gravel, shuffle out
in stocking-feet to breathe the gilded air.

Even the stars stand on alert
ready to rise or fall
at the moon's wane or whim.

Somewhere out there in wood or meadow
the Sand Hill Cranes bow down, the whitetail
deer will kneel

and I will write my psalm
to the sky-faring demigod moon.

Midnight River

The sky, stained dark as rumpled laundry,
grumbles at the thought of rising
to another day.

Thunder undercuts the morning's vigil
of sun rising, of mist burning off lakes.
Today the mists deepen, gather

like crows on a line, blot out the sun's
morning ritual of lift and stretch,
of day-brightening.

Even the ducks on the river are non-
descript gray, small ghost orbs
floating on the steel-wool water.

Another rumble and raindrops
splat across stained concrete,
drop like hollow notes

from distant piano keys.
A heavy foot holds down
the sustaining pedal.

Gifted water thrums
down the drainpipe, slithers
out onto the parched lawn.

Tomorrow the Real Work Begins

The dragonflies are thick in the meadow tonight,
a celebration for a job well done.

Up close they are deep periwinkle blue,
but against the sky they are a black outline,

an ink stamp. They rise and fall and rise
in unison, a single heartthrob.

I already feel as if I am leaving this place.
I stop on a patch of close-cropped grass,

spread arms with the dragonflies, raise
them higher in a salutation.

The sunset is growing pale behind me.
Before me the moon rises.

I wait for its fullness, its cold fire.
I will do my salutations to the moon

if there is no law against it.
Let those who worship morning salute the sun.

As for me, I am the night goddess, and tonight
I will hold the moon's full face in my palms.

Acknowledgments

The following poems appeared in *Lake Country Journal Magazine:* "The Leaf," "At the Museum," "Larger Than Life."

The poem "Munitions" was a featured poem in the online journal *On the Commons/Uncommon Words* (onthecommons.org/magazine/munitions).

The poem "Glove Lake Morning II" first appeared in a slightly different form in the journal *realgoodwords*.

The following poems appeared in *The Talking Stick Literary Journal:* "Cedar Waxwings," Down There," "Passing Thoughts," "What Holds Me," "Destroying Angel," "Just Now a Fish," "At the Exhibit," "Bakery Fresh."

The poem "Last Train Song" first appeared in the book *County Lines: 87 Minnesota counties, 130 Minnesota poets* (Loonfeather Press, 2008).

The poem "Off the Map" first appeared in the book *Fog and Woodsmoke: Behind the Image, Poems* (Lost Hills Books, 2011).

The poem "What Holds Me" is included in the book *The Heart of All that Is: Reflections on Home* (Holy Cow Press, 2013).

The poem "The Message" aired on Lakeland Public Television.

The poem "Spitting on Stones" aired on KAXE Radio's The Beat.

The following poems were included in the poetry chapbook *Diving the Drop-off: A Selection of Original Poetry* (self-published, 2006, 2012): "Cedar Waxwings," "The Leaf," "Perfect Is As," "At the Museum," "Destroying Angel," "Glove Lake Morning II," "Migraine."

The following poems were included in the poetry chapbook *Why I Keep Rabbits: New and Selected Poems* (self-published, 2010): "See the Child," "Rough Cut," "Benediction," "Why I Keep Rabbits," "At the Exhibit," "Bakery Fresh," "This Is the Poem."

The following poems were included in the chapbook *Writing from the Milkhouse: A Week on Madeline Island* (self-published, 2015): "The Generous Ones," "A Week On Madeline Island," "Putting By," "Digging for Truth," "A Good Night," "Tomorrow the Real Work Begins."

The poem "Munitions" was featured in the Franklin Art Center's Poetry on the Wall Exhibit and Books presented by the Crossing Arts Alliance in 2015.

The poems "Reunion Moon," "Night Burning," "Last Pocket" and "The Plot of Land" were included in Poetry On and Off the Wall Exhibits and Books presented by The Five Wings Arts Council in 2011 and 2012.

The following poems were awarded Honorable Mentions, Awards of Merit or Cash Prizes for First, Second or Third place in the annual League of Minnesota Poets Poetry Contest: "Aspiration," "If I Named You," "Scribbage" (under the title "Yahtzee"), "The Wheelchairs" (under the title "The Chairs"), "Other Rooms," "Glove Lake Morning II," "At the Exhibit," "Poem for Pablo," "Munitions."

The National Federation of State Poetry Societies Stevens Poetry Manuscript Competition

The National Federation of State Poetry Societies (NFSPS) is a nonprofit organization focused on poetry and education, which sponsors fifty annual poetry contests, the winners of which appear in the anthology *Encore*. NFSPS also sponsors the annual Stevens Poetry Manuscript Competition for the best collection of poems by a single poet. The contest winner receives a cash prize of $1,000, publication by NFSPS Press, and fifty copies of his or her prize-winning book. The annual deadline is October 15th, the decision is announced in January, and the prize-winning book is published in June. Complete submission guidelines are available from the NFSPS website at www.nfsps.com, where winning books and editions of *Encore* can be ordered.

Past Stevens Poetry Manuscript Competition Winners

2014
Beast, by Mara Adamitz Scrupe (Rochester Hills, MI: NFSPS Press, 2015). Judge: John Witte.

2013
Breaking Weather, by Betsy Hughes (Rochester Hills, MI: NFSPS Press, 2014). Judge: Glenna Holloway.

2012
Full Cry, by Lisa Ampleman (Rochester Hills, MI: NFSPS Press, 2013). Judge: Maggie Anderson.

2011
Good Reason, by Jennifer Habel (Rochester Hills, MI: NFSPS Press, 2012). Judge: Jessica Garratt.

2010
Lines from the Surgeon's Children, 1862-1865, by Rawdon Tomlinson (Rochester Hills, MI: NFSPS Press, 2011). Judge: Lola Haskins.

2009
Come In, We're Open, by Sara Ries (Rochester Hills, MI: NFSPS Press, 2010). Judge: Ralph Burns.

2008
Bear Country, by Dana Sonnenschein (Rochester Hills, MI: NFSPS Press, 2009). Judge: Carolyne Wright.

2007
Capturing the Dead, by Daniel Nathan Terry (Rochester Hills, MI: NFSPS Press, 2008). Judge: Jeff Gundy.

2006
The Meager Life and Modest Times of Pop Thorndale, by W. T. Pfefferle (Rochester Hills, MI: NFSPS Press, 2007). Judge: Patricia Fargnoli.

2005
Harvest, by Budd Powell Mahan (Rochester Hills, MI: NFSPS Press, 2006). Judge: Lawson Inada.

2004
Aqua Curves, by Karen Braucher (Rochester Hills, MI: NFSPS Press, 2005). Judge: Peter Meinke.

2003
The Zen Piano Mover, by Jeanne Wagner (Rochester Hills, MI: NFSPS Press, 2004). Judge: Ruth Berman.

2002
A Thousand Bonds: Marie Curie and the Discovery of Radium, by Eleanor Swanson (Rochester Hills, MI: NFSPS Press, 2003). Judge: Bruce Eastman.

2001
The Fine Art of Postponement, by Jane Bailey (Rochester Hills, MI: NFSPS Press, 2002). Judge: Donna Salli.

2000
The Stones for a Pillow, by Diane Glancy (Rochester Hills, MI: NFSPS Press, 2001). Judge: David Sutherland.

1999
Binoculars, by Douglas Lawder (Rochester Hills, MI: NFSPS Press, 2000). Judge: Kenneth Brewer.

1998
Singing in the Key of L, by Barbara Nightingale (Rochester Hills, MI: NFSPS Press, 1999). Judge: Sue Brannan Walker.

1997
Weighed in the Balances, by Alan Birkelbach (Austin, TX: Plainview Press, 1998). Judge: Anne Marx.

1996
Shadowless Flight, by Todd Palmer (Deerfield, IL: Lake Shore Publishing, 1997). Judge: Michael Bugeja.

1995
I Have Learned Five Things, by Elaine Christensen (Deerfield, IL: Lake Shore Publishing, 1996). Judge: Michael Dennis Browne.

1994
A Common Language, by Kathryn Clement (Deerfield, IL: Lake Shore Publishing, 1995). Judge: David Baker.

www.ingramcontent.com/pod-product-compliance
Lightning Source LLC
Chambersburg PA
CBHW071202090426
42736CB00012B/2422